CASTLE

" DOC IN LOCKUP"

U.S. NAVAL PRISON

━Edward T Duranty

Cover-South Cell Block circa 1930. USN No.147/30)

"THE CASTLE"

Fiction - Nonfiction - Some Facts – No Facts - No Proof - Some Proof – Lies –Some Truths – Reality Make Believe- Bunkum and Balderdash
Autobiography - Biography
 "Believe It or Not, Mr. Ripley."
 Sea Story -" This is no shit!"

No way could I be neutral in my feelings between an American combat soldier and an American that would NOT serve when his country asked him.

Pampered little draft dodgers were refusing to serve while the draft sent men to war that didn't have the resources, money, influence, or peer pressure from parents and relatives to connive a way out.

Please, Mr. Custer, I don't want to go."

They went, and they fought. Many were gravely injured, and so many gave their lives. Six months prisoners went home to collect state and government benefits, get laid, drink beer, and live a full life.

Successful connivers received a six months prison sentence (less for good behavior) sentenced to hard labor (you have to be kidding) and a Bad Contact Discharged.

Let us not forget the many intellectuals that jumped on the college deferment bandwagon. Hell, taking that way out, you could end up as the president of the United States!

I only reflect on the group of prisoners representing the "I don't want to go" movement. It does not reflex or involves real prisoners that committed real crimes and sentenced from years to life.

From the web origin unknown

Clarification.

The Portsmouth Naval Ship Yard is located in Portsmouth NH. The Naval Prison administratively is attached to the Naval Shipyard.

The prison is physically located in Kittery, Maine.

The name "U.S. Naval Prison" was changed to "U.S. Naval Disciplinary Command."

FROM THE AUTHOR (Doc)

In nineteen hundred and sixty-six, the Navy ordered that I report a tour of duty with the Third Marine Division in Vietnam.

As a Navy corpsman, it was indeed a cultural shock to leave the humdrum workday of a Naval Dispensary in Newport, R.I., to arrive at Camp Lejeune, North Carolina, to be re-tooled into a combat Marine Corpsman. (Squid to Jarhead.)

Gone were my thirteen button trousers, neckerchief, and a white hat. Upon arrival at Lejeune, they were replaced with Marine green apparel designed so I could run faster; live in for an undetermined length of time, with or without skivvies.

I relish the memories of singing the Marine Corps Hymn in the gas chamber with no mask, the no-neck drill sergeant doing five hundred "jumping jacks" without breaking a sweat. Crawling on my back under barbed wire while a machine gun fired overhead and mini explosives were erupting around me. It led me to keep asking?

"Am I a Marine yet?"

A memory that I will forever honor was walking under an archway at the entrance to Field Medicine School with a signboard that read.

"Under this archway walks the best Doc's in the world."
Chesty Puller

(365 Corpsmen died in the Vietnam War.)

Mock-up Vietnam villages had been erected to further the reality of our role in a combat operation. Mannequins with realistic war wounds exposed us to the actuality of the war that lies ahead.

Due to an extreme shortage of corpsmen in Vietnam, leave was not granted. Four of us rented a car and made it from Lejeune to Newport, RI and back before the plane left!

Boarding cattle cars to a nearby airport, we were on our way to "Nam."

Landing in Hawaii, we disembarked the aircraft while it refueled. Hawaiian Hula dancers came out on the runway dancing
in grass skirts, hanging strings of flowers around our necks.

The Gunny announced that Hawaii was the last stop, and it was an ideal time to bend over and kiss your ass goodbye.

My year in country was spent roaming along the

wilds of the Demilitarized Zone between North and South Vietnam; referred to as I Corps; it was not a fun place.

I was to find later in life that sleep was nearly impossible. The dreams of fright never go away, returning night after night.

Orders to the "Castle" - Navy Family Included.

It was a long road to the Castle both physically and mentally. Not only for me but also for my family.

I came home from a place where every morning when I awoke, I told myself, "I'll probably die tomorrow."

Upon my return, my family, with never-ending love, met me. The conquering hero returns, celebrations, daddy was home.

I knew from the start–go, I had a severe attitude adjustment to make.

"Pass the fucking bread."

Was not acceptable at the dinner table.

War affects all aspects of one's psychological being. Long separations win the top spot on the depression list. But wait! What about my family? I'm back home in a half-ass mental state, drinking too much, and doing my best to make up for the lost time.

Thus far, I captured all the attention. What about my wife and children? When the welcome home celebrations ended, I had to inform them of my orders, and we would be moving. The looks of dismay and hurt showed freely on their faces. A few tears were falling, and without comment, they turned and ran to their rooms.

That night after everything had been taken care of from dinner, my wife sat our children down to have them acknowledge and realize that we were a Navy family.

"Your father took an oath to defend our country. It is our duty as a military family to follow him with pride, dignity, and honor."

They accepted the explanations with the awareness that adversity and tribulations lay ahead. As a Navy family, we would meet and prevail over any and all obstacles that stand in our path.

As parents, we recognized their heartaches and sadness in being transferred. It is no easy task for young children to leave their school and friends with little knowledge of where they were going.

The questions start! Where are we going? Where will I be going to school? Will I have my own room? Will we know anybody? Is the dog going? My hamster? Can I take all my clothes? My CD? Is theTV going? Will they have cable? Is our telephone number the same? Is daddy going away on a ship?

It is not an easy task for a military family to up and move. The transfer to Kittery was especially challenging.

NAVY FAMILY ON THE MOVE

With my wife, three children, and a U-Haul trailer, we drove down Main Street in Kittery, Maine. Ten to twelve seconds later, Main Street ended.

Stopping at a service station, I filled up with gas and went inside to pay. I asked the attendant if I was anywhere near the Naval Prison?

He seemed to be amused to my asking for directions. Acknowledging, he answered the question with the most Down East accent I had ever heard.   Kittery, Maine

He corrected me immediately.

"It's called the Castle; if you don't refer to it as the Castle, no one will know what in hell you're talking about."

Answering my question, he informed me when I went over the next incline in the road, the Castle would be in plain view with the submarine base off to the right.

Arriving at a new duty station with a wife and children is not a piece of cake. We had to eat, sleep, and put a roof over our heads. When you're an enlisted man in the Navy, this part of the equation is you're on your own.

Don't get me wrong; the Navy did supply travel funds, household moving, and housing allowances. The lower your rank, the lower your benefits.

Naval Housing was available in Kittery, but no vacancies. For the first few months, we found temporary housing in Newmarket, NH.
It was a good twenty miles from Kittery.

The rental price and the expense of everyday travel wiped out our budget. McDonald's never had it so good.

We were notified that a unit in Admiralty Village was available. I accepted.

Admiralty Village is located at Kittery Point, on the shores of an Atlantic Ocean tributary.

The housing consisted of a single two-bedroom unit and several duplex two-family homes. We were signed to a single unit on Wilner Street.

I learned from neighbors in the village, the housing was constructed in the early nineteen forties in support of the shipyard and the submarine base.

Believe me, it looked it. Our unit resembled a cabin on the sea coast pelted by the ocean for thirty or forty years.

Their main characteristic was that they were not level. Over the years one end or the other of a unit had been slowly sinking into the ground. Consequently, the Navy deemed it unsuitable housing, and our monthly allowance for housing was lowered percentage-wise.

Moving in, we established living arrangements. Our interior was especially in need of painting. I complained to the maintenance staff and was issued two gallons of deep blue interior semi-gloss wall paint. We painted the entire inside, but our household furniture just never did fit in with the shiny blue walls.

What could you do? Move out? Go Where? Pease Air Force was only a few miles away. They had new base housing, but I
never heard of anyone from another service living there.

"Welcome to Admiralty Village, U.S. Naval Housing."

Our three children got to share and sleep in one small bedroom. The kitchen was small and efficiency sized, no yard, no garage, no storage shed, but, it was home.

Most of our belongings stayed packed in moving boxes piled to the ceilings.

We were well aware that complaints went to deaf ears. Navy wives had a way of keeping their sanity by bitching to each other.

Check off list:

Naval Disciplinary Command, Naval Submarine Base, Portsmouth Naval Ship Yard, Naval Hospital: Commissary-NO, Navy Exchange-NO, Enlisted Club- NO, (was a converted barracks where you could get a beer) Bowing Alley-NO, Gymnasium-NO, Thrift Store-NO, Daycare-NO, Package Store-NO, Movie Theater-NO.
Housing-YES

Single and Duplex units that were deficient, but in use. A few we noted were boarded up.

Check off list:

Pease Air Force Base,
 Seven miles from Admiralty Village.
All the NO Naval facilities listed above were YES at the Pease Air Force Base, including dependent housing and a nine-hole golf course.

Military families were authorized to use their facilities. Still, I found the logistics of base security, club membership requirements, and resenting the Air Force because I joined the Navy, we shopped elsewhere.

The children were admitted to various area schools and began the process of making new friends. It was a struggle for them being crowded into one small room, but we made adjustments and adapted to the hardships. We were a Navy Family.

The year we left Admiralty Village conditions hadn't changed. We wondered if the next family would appreciate the walls painted in a dark semi-gloss blue!

I don't know what happened to Admiralty Village, if it was torn down, added on to, or still the pits!

I found this interesting article in the local Portsmouth paper dated 1974.

MILITARY FAMILIES "WANT TO CRY" OVER ADMIRALTY VILLAGE HOUSING CONDITIONS.

KITTERY, Maine — Black mold that causes asthma and headaches in children and adults. Cracks in the walls. Water dripping from ceiling light fixtures. Outdated appliances that leak gas. These are several of a litany of concerns raised by residents of Admiralty Village, home to nearly 200 military families who work at Portsmouth Naval Shipyard and in other military capacities on the Seacoast. Four residents, all active-duty military or military wives whose names are not being revealed as they are concerned about repercussions, met with Seacoast officials recently to talk about what they called "horrid" living conditions. With them, they brought surveys filled out by another 22 residents — some who had positive experiences at Admiralty Village. Still, most of whom painted a bleak picture of life at the military housing complex. In all, the residents detailed an aging and substandard apartment complex that has had little or no internal remodeling and existed on "Band-Aids upon Band-Aids. With apartments too small under military housing standards, the management turned a deaf ear to requests for repairs and potentially serious health hazards from mold and mildew conditions.

Balfour Beatty Communities, the real estate services company that owns and operates Admiralty Village under contract with the U.S. Navy said it understands concerns have been raised and intends to begin interior renovations starting in two years.

But the military members or their spouses said many of these problems should have been dealt with long ago. "The men and women who serve our country shouldn't be living in deplorable conditions like this," said Raquel, who asked that her real name not be used. "We should be treated more respectfully. No one should live this way."

One year at the prison, and I requested that my shore duty be terminated and that I will be transferred to sea duty. I was transferred to the USS ALBANY (CG-10), homeported in Mayport, Florida.

Packed up, on the road again, a Navy family on the move. Housing was no problem, Navy Housing was a far cry from Kittery, private housing was plenteous and affordable. We acquired a three-bedroom home at Jacksonville Beach a few miles from the Mayport Navy base at Jacksonville Beach. The house had a large private backyard and an attached garage. We walked to the beach!

To coin an old phrase.

"It was liked we died and went to heaven."

There was one small catch! The owner was moving to New Jersey for a job-related advancement and would return at the end of three years. I would be transferred at the same exact time. The catch, we had to take care of her cat, "Thomas."

We had lived there for well over a year when Thomas disappeared. He did not return. After three months, I called the owner and explained the situation. She was heart-broken.

Nearing the end of our third year, early morning, my wife opened the kitchen door, and Thomas walked in like "where's my bowl?"

I have strayed a long way from the title of this book. I wanted to share with you a few experiences that every military family deals with in the service of our country.

Chapter 1

When we drove past the prison, for once, there was complete silence in the car. The prison was huge and ugly. Now we knew why everyone called it the "Castle." The only thing missing was a moat, drawbridge, and tubs of hot oil being spilled from the rooftops.

Before arriving, we had researched the prison on the internet. The flag was raised on April 11, 1908. The Naval Prison was commissioned under the command of the United States Marine Corps It soon acquired the nickname of "Alcatraz of the East." There must be volumes of literature concerning the many souls that were incarcerated inside the walls. During the Second World War, the inmate count exceeded three thousand prisoners. Just how in the hell did I end up stationed here? I am not a reformer or a goody-two-shoes. If a guy is in the slammer, he has to answer for his actions. It is that simple. The family settled in, my leave over, it was time to report for duty. The prisons main gate spanned over and across the roadway. A center section opened and closed for vehicles. One walkthrough gate was located on the side entrance of the security building. Standing outside, I counted three Marine sentries. No doubt, I was getting the once over. Dressed in a white Navy uniform, neckerchief, and a white hat. I could well imagine their conversation. "What in the hell does that squid want?" I was gravely wrong; the medical caduceus on my uniform sleeve was observed, along with my combat ribbon with the Marine Corp emblem and two stars. I was heartily welcomed. I felt cool; I was back with the Grunts. Gaining entry to the inside was not easy. Escorted to the Personnel Office, I was given a chair and asked to sit. I turned over my service records and was immediately informed of the mission and functioning of the prison. Rules and regulations came. Next, the handouts never ended. With each step of the "welcome aboard," a staff member would appear to warn me sternly that a prison is a dangerous place. "This is the house of bad guys, when you are in here, be alert! The inmates will approach you, smile, and maybe even try to befriend you." "WAKE UP! Realize they hate your guts. If given their choice, they would stomp your ass into the ground and then piss on you." "WHY? Because you're the good guy, you're the guy that landed them in this shit hole. You follow the rules; you're the ass hole. Being new, you will be inundated with sob stories, tales of injustices, guard abuse, and a multitude of prisoners rabble bullshit." "Always keep a visual picture in your mind to the possibility of spontaneous uncertainty in the prison environment. Be vigilant and always attentive to your exact prison location. Never place

yourself in a position where you are alone in the company of an inmate.
If that situation occurs, immediately take whatever means are available, to remove yourself from the area, and away from the inmate."
The prisoners are under complete surveillance and have little or no freedom to respond for what they suppose are the injustices prefabricated against them. Convicts have found ways to retaliate in every prison in
the world. The prison grapevine is a way of communication that transmits rumors, warnings, news, gossip, and secret code to every inmate in the institution. It was sort of like back when the telephone had party lines, and the whole neighbor listened in. Your mother knew everything. The highest aspiration of an inmate is to compromise a guard or staff member into a small concession. Maybe sneak in a candy bar, mail a letter, no big thing, nothing more than a little "favor!" Being a nice guy, you are soon found out. An inmate snitch drops a dime on your ass, and you find yourself facing military justice. For the inmate, it was a winning day. He proved you a loser. Rack one up for the bad guys. The score? 1 for the inmates, 0 for the guards. Tomorrow the game continues, inmates against the guards, twenty-four seven, three hundred and sixty-five days a year. During my

welcome aboard briefing, I remember two distinct topics that remain active in my memory to this very day. I'm not sure who brought up the issues, whether it was one of the briefing staff or one of the marine clerks working in the office. If taken a hostage, at that very moment, I would be considered deceased. There would be no communication, involving discussions or negotiations between the inmates and prison officials. An immediate altercation would go down by a specially trained unit of marines, using live ammunition and lethal force to silence all opposition and neutralize the area ASAP! I believe I signed a document that I understood the implications if taken as a hostage. My wife does remember that I brought papers home for her to sign that she understood the consequences if I was held, hostage.

Chapter 2

The prisoners on their arrival were well informed that fatal force would be the immediate response to the holding of a hostage.
I have wondered if the prisoners not considered enemy forces, took hostages thus becoming subservient, and could warrant the protection of the Geneva Accords.

The second topic of interest was a printed diagram showing the perimeter of the prison grounds. The bulk of the security fencing ran along the backside of the prison in line with the Piscataquis River. Guard towers were well placed and manned 24-7 by Marines with live ammunition.

The river flowed between Seavey's Island and Pierce Island and ran its course to the Atlantic Ocean. It was classified as one of the swiftest rivers in the world. Well known for its fast flow and treacherous currents. One of the reasons it was known as East Alcatraz.

Liken to the fast-moving currents and undertows of the San Francisco Bay, there is no record of any inmate escaping by swimming across the channel. There was a yarn that, in earlier times, an inmate gave it a try. Realizing the current was too strong, he turned and swam back to the prison. The tale goes that he was shot dead as he struggled out of the water. Prison grapevine folklore at its best.

The basic word given to a prisoner was if you touch the fence in any manner, you will be shot. I talked to Marine guards, who said they would not hesitate to shoot.

A widespread inmate discussion.

"Would they really shoot?"

Standard answer.

"Touch the fence and see."

I was told that no prisoner ever touched the fence! From the Records Office, I was ushered in and out to meet the Executive Officer, a Navy Commander, and the Commanding Officer, a Marine Colonel. A formality to meet new enlisted arrivals, as in all probabilities, we would not meet again.

The formal check-in being over, a marine guard showed me the way to the sixth floor, the domicile of the Medical Department.

In a real castle, the stairway steps are around five feet long, a foot wide and a good eight inches up to the next level. There were no deviations of the prison steps. Sick Bay was on the top floor, six floors up. The day I checked in the elevator was working, the guard informed me there would be many days when it would be out of order.

Laughingly he told me when I did the first climb, my knees would feel like jelly. He was right.

The sickbay open area was about the size of a half basketball court. It was basically lined with chairs for when the prisoners were treated or interviewed in groups. From the outer perimeter of the circle were rooms that were used for a lab, x-rays, and record keeping.

Two psychiatrists and one psychologist occupied three office rooms.

A more extensive treatment room was located just outside of the lines of chairs. All medical medications, syringes/needles, and an assortment of surgical instruments were kept under lock and key inside a large metal security cabinet.

Two medical doctors each occupied a side office directly off the treatment room. The psychologist was a civilian, but the rest of the crew was all Navy. Six to eight corpsmen were assigned for the primary care and treatment of inmates, sanitary conditions, safety issues, and other general health issues. Their charge was in maintaining a highly healthy environment for the well being of the prisoners.

Returning from the shit of Vietnam, I had vivid memories of the pain and trauma that afflicted combat marines and sailors.

Now it was expected that I should have the same compassion and concern toward some draft dodging son-of-a-bitch. I was an almost Nurse, but not bound by the Hippocratic oath. However, the caduceus on my uniform reminded me that my job was to care for the sick and injured. No exceptions.

The inmate's prison uniform, gray in color, consisted of long-legged trousers and a pullover shirt. The letters CMP in large black letters were indelibly displayed across the ass of the pants. CMP meaning, "Court Martial Prisoner." For the remainder of the book, I will intersperse that designation.

Seven to eight prisoners were assigned to sickbay as part of their work detail. Most of these inmates were "lifers" and thought to be the most trustworthy. Other phraseology for a lifer might encompass; murderer, killer, rapist, child molester, sexual pervert, thief and all other terminology listed under the heading of "Scumbag."

They made up a lesser percentage of the total prison population. Lifers would spend most of their lives behind bars. When they exhausted their military appeals, they would be transferred to a prison in their home state or possibly to the Army prison at Fort Leavenworth, Kansas.

The truth of the matter was that they were exceptional model prisoners. If a lifer had a chance of parole after thirty or forty years, his most valuable resource would be a history of perfect conduct during his entire incarceration.

CMP's that were found guilty of perpetrating crimes against the general population, and arrested by civilian law enforcement, were generally turn over to the military for trial, sentencing, and punishment.

The sentences for these type crimes, robbery, car theft, extortion, drug involvement, assaults, etc. could result in serving two to ten-year sentences. After appeals, an inmate with time still remaining to serve would be discharged other than honorable and transferred to a civilian prison.

A majority of the CMP lock-ups were Vietnam related. Men who had completed a year in Vietnam and refused to return for a second tour. Or while in-country were guilty of insubordination, war crimes, or committed violations against the mandates of the Geneva Conventions.

Recruits completing military training and civilians subject to the draft that was right out rejecting going to Vietnam or serving any form of active duty had a choice of three roads in which to travel. (1) Buy their way-out by arranging for a college deferment (Sound familiar?) (2) Denounce their American citizenship and apply for exile in Canada. (3) Commit a semi-serious offense against the Uniform Code of Military Justice. Nothing serious, go AWOL for a week, punch out your superior, smoke some dope, steal from your shipmates, or offer sexual services.

Rebellion proved the popular way to go. The verdict of a special court-martial followed the norm of six months in prison and a Bad Conduct Discharged. Appalling choice? Maybe, but one's life has its priority.

If I considered the priority of my own life after being in receipt of orders back to Vietnam, would I contemplate one of the three choices? You bet your ass I would. My final pick would be number (4). Go back!

Marines returning from duty in Vietnam were re-assigned to new duty stations. One such station was guard duty at the Naval Disciplinary Command, in Kittery, Maine. Knowing with each day, they could receive orders returning them to Vietnam had the unfortunate assignment to guard marines and sailors, who chose a six months prison sentence rather than serve.

During the prison's day-to-day routine, incidents were bound to occur. Generally, most were minor infractions committed by CMP's infringing on the rules. CMP gang leaders retaliated by orchestrating encounters against unfavorable guards.

Did I say? "Gang leaders!"

It is a straightforward fact that gangs never existed within the walls of the Naval Prison. Did they? Did they not? I will leave that up to you, but for me, they did.

Chapter 3

A prison guard writes up three or four CMP's for infractions. They lose their privileges for a week. They bitch; same old story the guard has it in for them.

As a medical corpsman (non-combatant), I could not be involved with the operational functions of the guards, mission. I probably heard more prisoner conversations than the prison priest.

Follow this lead! The prison guard noted for his eagerness to put CMP's on report is standing his duty watch at the entrance to the prison library.

A CMP approaches the guard, and without having first asked permission, to speak he mouths off.

"Word is that you're going back to Vietnam, this time you will be going home in a metal box!"

The remark was deliberately made by the CMP for no other reason than to agitate and unnerve the guard. He was successful

The reaction was instant, with the guard flustered and discouraged, screaming profanities into the CMP's face.

Standing at attention, staring straight ahead, the CMP displayed a widely smirking smile, hoping to entice the guard further.

Extensive training kept the guard from engaging in any sort of physical contact.

Laying hands on a CMP was a court-martial offense. Knowing that the CMP was striving for physical confrontation the
guard radioed for help.

The response was immediate. A squad of specially trained Marines, known as the "Chasers," descended on the CMP. Roughly forcing him down until his face laid flat against the cement floor.

Using a light rope, they tied his legs together and both arms behind his back. Shrieking obscenities at the Chasers, his head was yanked upward and a gag crammed into his mouth.

Bodily the Chasers lifted the CMP to their shoulders, carrying him to a segregated holding cell. He was roughly laid face up on a solid metal slab, a third smaller than his prison bedding.

Told to keep his fucking eyes shut, the Chasers engaged in an onslaught of verbal warnings, any disobedience bullshit, would lead to very unfriendly attitude adjustments.

The prison disciplinary board would review the charges against the CMP. True to form, most offenses of this nature resulted in thirty days lost of all privileges and ten days piss and punk in the hole. (Bread and water-solitary confinement.)

Two separate outcomes would result from the incident. The guard would not forget the CMP, and when the time was right, the son-of-a-bitch would learn about "payback."

The CMP, once finishing his confinement, would return among his fellow CMP's as a returning hero. His statue among the inmates significantly increased. On the grapevine, he was known as the "man" who put the screws to a guard.

It doesn't end there. After getting out of the hole, the CMP shows up every morning for sick call. Complaining to the doctor that the guards were out to get him. So scared that he is thinking suicide.

Three or four mornings of treating the CMP, the doctor gets fed up and sends him to see one of the psychiatrists. In a short time, has the CMP's privileges restored, twice a week follow up appointments, and a prescription for an anti-depressant medication.

Each morning the CMP would be excused from his work detail and sent to sickbay for his medication. Depending on how long the line was, he copped two to three hours a day free time.

When it's his turn for medication. He opens his mouth wide, and a pill is inserted to the back of his throat. Given a cup of water, he rinses the inside of a closed mouth and swallows. Finished, he opens his mouth wide once again. A thin wooden depressor is used to move his tongue about to ensure the pill was swallowed. No matter how though the exam, a CMP would fake his swallow, conceal the pill, leave and deliver it to his gang leader. He, in turn, used it to obtain contraband, favors, and maybe dealing with a guard.

Give this a thought! Is it possible that a gang leader orchestrated the whole incident between the CMP and the guard?

The animosity between the two factions persevered each and every day. The shit never ends.

Chapter 4

The old days, prisoners hauling cask circa 1908. Notice Guard with rifle. Credit: Naval History and Heritage Command/8158

Just how stressful is being sentenced to six months of hard labor at the Naval Prison, Kittery, Maine? I personally say its like a piss hole in the snow compared to twelve months of mud fucking in the jungles of Vietnam. In hindsight, no one could ever remember a CMP dying while serving out his sentence!

The typical six months CMP is in his early twenties with the mentality that all government officials, military personnel, and law enforcement are a bunch of assholes.

Inside the walls, the CMP is as humble as apple pie. Quick to give me justification of why they were incarcerated:

COURT-MARTIAL PRISONER

1. "I finished High School, my grades were top shelf. I was a basketball star; the chicks loved me. When I turned eighteen, my parents bought me a new car. It came with a no-limit credit card, and the future of being accepted by Yale University was looking real good. Then came the fucking Draft!"

2. "I hated school and every miserable bastard teacher in the place. When I turned sixteen, I told them to shove it. Got a job at the Burger King. I got the girl I worked with pregnant. Her family flipped out. I got drafted. She moved in with my drunken old man. Test results reflected that I would best be suited in the Infantry as
a rifleman, I told them to go fuck themselves."

3. "I did a year with the grunts in I Corps, Vietnam, and have no idea how in the hell I survived. All around me, my buddies were being blown to hell in chunks and pieces. I took a bullet in my left leg, missed the bone, healed up, and I was awarded the Purple Heart. Eight months back in the states, and I got orders to Vietnam for another year. I made a decision! I'm not fucking going."

4. "My father was a drunken son-of-a-bitch who's pleasure was kicking the shit out of my mother and me. Home on boot leave I buried a kitchen knife in his chest! The bastard lived, didn't press charges, but I got six and a kick for being AWOL!

I loved these tales of woe. Were they true? I think not. A lifer told me they were using me as a rehearsal before they saw the shrink.

The sad part of conversing with CMP's was the realization that they truly believed they didn't owe their country a damn thing much less die for it.

I relish creating a scene.
I would ask you to keep this one in mind as you continue to read "The Castle."

A young Marine crouched in a wet, muddy hole has covered himself with his poncho trying to keep some of his body parts dry from the monsoon rains. He eats from a small box of C-rations. Using his
John Wayne, he carefully removes the lid of a small tin can wishing above all that its contents would yield fruit cocktail. In the dark, his sense of touch tells him that it's fucking pound cake again. The heavy rain restricts his vision, he can't see if the enemy is probing or under the wire. He hears the sound of Viet Cong mortar's leaving their tubes followed by shouts of "Incoming." Scared as shit, he tries to burrow deeper in his hole.

0500 The CMP is pissed. It's five o'clock in the morning, and the guards are on his ass to move it. Thirty minutes to wash, get dressed, and junk on the bunk. Having the routine down to a science, it only takes a few minutes to arrange all of his possessions, neatly on his tightly made bunk.

0530 Falling in formation, they walk a yellow painted line leading to the mess hall. There are yellow lines throughout the prison in which prisoners must walk on when moving about.

Shoulder to shoulder, eyes starring straight ahead, they step out toward the mess hall. No talking, no facial expressions, step off the yellow line expect an ass chewing and a cold breakfast.

Entering the mess hall, each CMP is given three pieces of silverware and a metal tray. Holding his tray out, he is ushered by the serving line where another CMP ("Please Mr. Custer I don't want to go") doles out his breakfast.

A guard directs him to a table and chair where he is told to sit and eat. Five to seven minutes later, the guard running the show indicates to the CMP he has finished his breakfast by pointing to the way out.

A guard counts the CMP's silverware, has him drop them into a container of water, scrapes his tray clean, and is ordered to return to his position on the yellow line.

Reading a posted menu, he notes the noon meal dessert is fruit cocktail. "Again!"

The CMP gets three wholesome meals a day. The mess hall is run under the supervision of a Marine staff. Preparation, serving, and cleaning is done by CMP labor.

Staff members have their own mess hall located on the first floor of the prison. It is overseen and operated by active-duty Navy and Marine food service personnel. The entire first floor, without exception, is off-limits to all CMP's.

The two separate mess halls prevented the staff mess from the danger of possible retaliation by contamination. An inmate working in the staff preparation kitchen could introduce toxic organisms into the meal being prepared. A foodborne Illness would be disastrous to catastrophic for the Marine guards to maintain the security of the prison.

Returned to his cell or a dormitory, the CMP finds his mattress overturned, and his possessions scatted about on the floor. The message? You failed inspection!

The cellblock went up four tiers, with over three hundred individual cells. If a CMP refused to work at an assigned detail, he lost most privileges, confined his meals brought to him. The cells on the top tier were exclusively kept for homosexuals.

Open cells held the rest of the general population except for a fraction who were assigned to one of the two dormitories. They were housed with two-man upper and lower type bunks and a small non-lockable locker for each inmate. CMP's assigned to either dormitory were either suck asses, favorites of a guard, an old buddy form an earlier duty station or even an acquaintance higher up in the administration.

Ever substantiated was the fact that CMP gang leaders retained control over inmates assigned to dormitories.

Yes, there were gangs! The enlisted marine guards were probably well aware but practiced the age-old policy of see nothing and say nothing. To get involved could lead to being a private for the next three years.

CMP gang leaders bludgeon CMP's into being workers, servants, sweethearts, and hard-core enforcers. The enforcers used physical force to persuade non-conforming CMP's to join the fold. The gang quietly and secretly dealt in contraband, drugs, sex, and fear. How did I know so much about gang activity?
 Prison psychiatrists in their superior wisdom established a program mandating staff members, including hospital corpsmen, would be assigned two CMP's and act as their counselors. Great program? Hard to believe a CMP wanted to talk rehabilitation with an active duty lifer? The CMP's

were given a promise by the psychiatrists that all conversations would be held confidential, with the counselor being fully aware of that fact. Would corpsmen swap juicy information with each other? No way!

For one hour, it was sit back and listen to a CMP pour out his inner being. Divulging gang activity, latest rumors from the prison grapevine, the stupidity of the guards, and how fucked up the prison was run.

My CMP's would shoot their mouths off about anything and everything. It was a piece of cake to maneuver the CMP into babbling everything he knew about gang activity.

An hour in sickbay was an hour away from their prison environment. My thought was the program was a chain puller, a waste of time. Counseling should be left to those trained and qualified to do so.

During a session with one of my CMP's the Marine Sentry stationed at the entrance to sickbay ushered a CMP into the treatment room. It was unusual; typically, a corpsman would do the escorting. The prison doctor, was of Mexican descent, met the CMP who was also Mexican. Taking the CMP by the arm, he led him into his office. Closing his door behind him, the doctor had sidestepped the policies of checking in and recording the CMP's name, complaint, time, etc. My assigned CMP, who had also been watching, abruptly interrupted me whispering.

"That's him, he's the main man, has four leaders that report to him plus two boyfriends, one sleeps on the top bunk above him."

After a guard took charge of the CMP, I waited around in the treatment room until the door opened and the doctor escorted the CMP out to the guard station. The CMP was well built, perhaps in his late twenties. They spoke in Spanish, and it pissed me off that I couldn't understand. Of all people, the doctor knew that only English was to be expressed inside the prison.

I reported the incident to my supervisor, who informed me for my own well being to accept as fact, that in this prison, there are no gangs or gang leaders.

A simple concept to accept, and I did.

Photo by Lena Shearer

Chapter 5

The main cellblock being somewhere near three hundred and fifty individual cells awaited new arrivals. The top tier was exclusively reserved for homosexuals.

"If you were queer, you came here." To confess that your interest was on your shipmate's ass was a sure ticket for six months and a Bad Conduct Discharge.

By the time one of the prisons shrinks figured out if the inmate was or wasn't queer, he had finished his sentence and was long gone.

No longer did he have to work in an engine room staying at a hundred and fifteen degrees, no washing pots and pans for months on end, no hanging over the
side painting with lead ingredient paint's and, most importantly, no Vietnam!

Could it get any better? With good time, you served less than six months. Three meals a day, movie time, and a prison made dark blue suit. Plus! A free bus ticket to your home of record, twenty-five dollars cash, and escorted to a bus in downtown Portsmouth, New Hampshire.

It always didn't quite go that way. Anytime during the releasing process, to sitting in the bus station, you get smart and give the guard some shit!

Back you went to the Castle. You could expect to do another thirty days, plus no time is given for good behavior.

Once the bus driver took the inmate's ticket, and he was seated, it marked the end of his confinement.

UNLESS, he got off the bus!

Inmates' release mainly dwelled on administrative procedures. Without a CMP wanting to spend another week or two at the Castle, the process worked well with little or no interruptions.

The inmate's arrival at the Castle was quite a different story. Prisoners from various Navy and Marine bases throughout- out the world were airlifted by the Air Force to Pease Air Force Base, just outside of Portsmouth, New Hampshire.

The prisoner's great awaking came when well after midnight they were deplaned to the runway. I was assigned to the welcoming detail to provide medical assistance if needed.

Before leaving the prison, I was advised by the department administrator to the fact that the prison doctors were concerned over the number of prisoners arriving with ankle injuries. I was to observe and to report any reckless injuries caused directly by the guards.

Having a very close relationship with the guards, I mentioned to the Sergeant in charge, my orders.

"No sweat Doc, I'll take care of it."

A statement like that coming from a Marine Sergeant can make you start to worry!

We arrived in the prison bus approximately thirty minutes before the plane landed. We were directed to the runway where the passengers would be deplaned. They would be greeted by a well trained Marine welcome squad. Each Marine being six feet or taller, weighing in at over two hundred pounds, and were referred to as "Chasers."

The new arrivals were hustled out of the airplane and formed into what could be called a semblance of a military line.

The officer in charge of the prisoners made a count and then turned a list of names over to the Marine Sergeant. His responsibility over, his crew re-boarded the plane.

The Chasers stood watching and waiting until the plane had taxied some distance away. The prisoners were now official inmates of the Naval Prison. (Naval Disciplinary Command)

The new arrivals stood shuffling about complaining about not getting anything to eat or drink, and it was too damn cold to be standing on the runway.

As the bitching carried on the Chasers took up a stance directly, and behind each prisoner. In unison, the prisoners felt a large hand clamp down on the back of their necks, followed by a sharp squeezing pain.

With an exerted movement forward, the Chaser's boot kicked the prisoner's ankle outward, forcing the legs apart. Intensified pressure on the back of the prisoner's neck accompanied by a robust downward shove strong-armed the prisoner into a spread-eagle stance, unable to move.

The Chasers boot blows against the prisoner's ankles were persuasive and forceful. As if the Sergeant was reading my mind, he turned and gave me thumbs up.

Watching the Chasers immobilizing the prisoners, I wasn't about to shirk my duty. To this day, I can honestly say I never saw any blood.

While a prisoner was being held in an unmovable position, he was thoroughly padded down. The prisoners had been stripped searched before they were transferred, then again before boarding the aircraft.

The Sergeant placed a cardboard box down in front of the line. As the Chasers found contraband, the Sergeant tossed it into the box. It was hard to believe, but when they finished, the box was two thirds full.

Body searches over, the Chasers still maintained a handgrip on the back of each prisoner's neck. The Chaser, raising his arm in a hard thrust upwards, propelled the prisoner upright to a standing position. Made to stand at attention, they were told to keep their fucking eyes looking straight ahead.

Releasing the holds on the prisoner's necks, the Chasers turning in unison took up a stance directly in front of each prisoner. The Chasers went eye to eye with the prisoner with both faces only inches a part. The chasers harassed the prisoner with a flurry of articulated obscenities dwelling on the prisoner's liking for young boys.

When it was apparent that none of the prisoners was going to lose control, freak out or resist, they were singly ordered to board the prison bus.

If I thought the Pease runway reception was awesome, it didn't hold a candle to the bus ride back to the prison. The jawing increased to a level where no one could be heard.

Chasers raced up and down the bus aisle, pushing the prisoners into seats, cursing at them to put their god damn hands on top of the seat in front of them and rest their heads face down on their two arms.

Fuck up, and your goddam fingers will be smashed.

Bellowing vulgarities at any prisoner who moved. Chasers were up and down the aisle shouting curses to maintain their seating positions, or the bus would be stopped, the offender took outside to get his ass kicked.

I sat quietly in the front of the bus, trying to imagine what thoughts must be going through the minds of these prisoners. Up until their arrival, they had been confined in brigs that often had perks for good behavior. The worse part was being limited, but many Brigs usually allowed model prisoners to work on details outside of the compound. For them; possession of contraband was relatively easy to come by.

Did these prisoners have the idea that the prison would operate similarly? I was confident that memories of their brig perks and favors were long gone, replaced with a real sense of identity loss, fused with shame, and a lack of self-confidence.

Chasers banging nightsticks, and yelling obscenities refused to allow the prisoners to even think about moving. Muscle spasms were becoming so intense that prisoners were close to mental and physical collapses.

I stood up and made eye contact with the Sargent to inform him that the situation was out of hand. He had to order the Chasers to relax the prisoner's positions. He gave me a wink!

Just then, the bus passed through the main gate and came to a stop in the prison yard. A Chaser's loud voice boomed out from the back of the bus.

"Hands down, sit back, anyone, and I mean anybody looks other than straight ahead will be one sorry son-of-a-bitch."

No one looked elsewhere. Every prisoner on the bus felt instant relief to their shoulders, arms, and back pains. It was perfect timing. I came to realize that the Pease detail and the trip back was well planned. To the Marine Chasers, the trip was just another same old

I wondered if I had given the Sergeant the word to relax the prisoners if he would have done it? I never asked and will never know.

There was no physical brutally. If a prisoner thought out the reality of his situation, he would have reconciled that the mistreatment or abuse he was sustaining was verbal.

Not one prisoner complained of having been sick or in pain nor requested my assistance. They let the guard's verbal crapola along with implied threats, conjured up the fear of uncertainty.

In all probability, the Chasers were repeating phrases and insults that were bestowed upon them by their boot camp drill instructors. If foul language is acceptable for boot camp, it can't be out of place in a prison.

Verbal abuse has its purpose. New arrivals that resisted or clashed with the Chasers were classified as aggressive and confrontational. Processing is delayed, and the prisoner is confined to a locked cell. The results of behavioral evaluations will determine the severity and safety of his confinement.

When the bus came to a stop, the Chasers were shouting at the prisoners.

"Out!" "Out!" "Out!"

Chapter 6

Struggling to get out of their seats, the prisoners shoved and squeezed each other, trying to force their way to the front. The exit door backed up. The chasers screamed at the prisoners to move forward. The pushing caused several of the prisoners to lose their balance, stumble out, and fall to the pavement.

With cries of urgency, the Chasers ran the prisoners through an entrance to six-foot cement steps leading to the top floor. Forced to run, guards stationed along the stairway, pounded on the cement steps with nightsticks yelling profanities and urging them on.

When a prisoner fell, he was pulled to his feet with loud threats of getting his ass kicked if he didn't keep going. Falling again,
he would be left to crawl the rest of the way.

Dog-tired, crying from exhaustion and suffering from painful leg cramps, most managed to reach the top floor. Hustled into a large gym-type room and were ordered to stand in a yellow-painted square, at attention, looking straight ahead and keep their fucking mouths shut.

Some so exhausted that they were unable to stay on there square. They were the victims of increased harassment.

It was by no means a somber scene, it was somewhat hostile. I have come to learn that there is no such phenomenon as Marines having "quiet time."

As each inmate took a stance in his yellow square, he got his ear full of just what a sorry son-of-a-bitch he was.

When all the yellow squares were filled, a prison trustee placed a cardboard box and marking pencil in front of each square.

The order was given.

"Strip to your birthday suit. Put all clothing in the box in front of you. Record your name and serial number on the label provided and paste it the top of the box, you have five minutes get to it!"

The trustees quickly gathered up the boxes up and left. The prisoners were informed that their possessions would be kept in storage and returned to them when they were released.

The result was a group of bare-ass lost souls standing at attention inside their designated yellow squares. The Welcoming ritual was the primary purpose for my presence. Stepping aside, the Marine Sergeant relinquished control of the group explaining that Doc would conduct primary examinations to ensure that no asshole was bringing crabs into the prison.

I want to make it quite clear that corpsmen assigned to the prison took the medical screening of incoming prisoners very seriously. In the event of a medical emergency, a doctor was called to assist. The Portsmouth Naval Hospital was less than a mile away.

Tongue depressor in hand, I would have the prisoner open his mouth, hold his tongue down, and examine the inside of the mouth and throat while having the prisoner saying "ah."

That was not good enough for the Sergeant; he insisted that the prisoner increase the sound of his "ah's" until he could hear it from the opposite side of the room. This might of amused him, but I was the one being showered with spit.

With the medical examinations over the Trustee's again appeared with clothing and toiletry articles for each prisoner. With the completion of this phase, they would be birthed and fed. The hoopla shouting and vocal harassment would soon be history. However, it didn't go away, the Sergeant had the final say.

Welcome to the U.S. Naval Disciplinary Command, don't fuck up!"

Chapter 7

The majority of the prisoners wanted to do there time and move on. However, in every barrel of apples, there are always a small number of rotten ones.

I never knew there was a Naval Prison. I quizzed a large number of Sailors and Marines that were on active duty before 1974 if they knew where the Naval Prison was located? Nearly all were unaware that there was a Navy Prison and no idea of its geographical location. It was one duty station you didn't ever want to know about unless like the unluckiest of us all got orders to report there.

After morning breakfast, a CMP followed a pretty well-repeated routine. He would report to his work detail, read incoming mail, use the library, and maybe put in a request for visitation.

If a CMP did not want to work the cellblock provided him home with meals served in, but only entitled to a few privileges.

CMP's were assigned to various details depending on their interest and willingness to work. The most substantial identities were the clothing factory, woodworking shop, and the maintenance division. Smaller shops were available to CMP's desiring to learn the basics of a specific occupation.

The clothing factory-fabricated dark blue suit coats and trousers for the day a CMP would be given twenty-five dollars and put on a bus. Black ties were optional. Actually, when cut loose, a CMP didn't look bad at all, except for the burlap that lined the inside of his suit coat, a white shirt with an extra-large neck size and wearing double-wide black shoes.

For reasons unexplained, I never had accessibility or cause to enter any prison workspace. The prison psychiatrists heartily supported the CMP's day in and day out work Schedules. It provided for the maturity and healthy growth of the inmate's ideology, thus aiding his return to society as a useful citizen. Perhaps, even take your daughter to her senior prom.

My duty nights were on the sixth floor in sickbay. The door was locked on the outside by a Marine guard stationed on the outside entrance foyer.

In an emergency, the word was radioed to the sentry on the floor. I was alerted by phone. A typical call would transpire between two and three o'clock in the morning.

"A suicide in progress!"

It was a good run down five flights of stairs knowing full well it would be a false alarm.

To my knowledge, a CMP never did do himself in. It made no sense, a few months, and he would be on his way home. The story behind most attempted suicides was entertainment.

"Watch Doc run."

Once I deemed the inmate was no threat to himself. I made the return trip up six flights of stairs to wait for the next call.

One recreational escape, from the daily humdrum of serving time, was for CMP's to persuade a psychiatrist or one of the medical doctors into prescribing a mood stabilizer. Psychiatric drugs were given to inmates diagnosed with symptoms touching on a probable psychological disorder.

You could easily spot CMP's on drugs by their swaggering about, eyes rolling, and sporting shit-eating grins. It was all a sham to convince fellow inmates that they were high and made it known they were nobody to mess with. Acquiring a stash, a CMP could become a known dealer trading his goodies with other prisoners for illegal

contraband. I'm sure he "coughed" up a few for his gang leader.
No way could this happen! The medication was placed in the CMP's mouth by medical personnel and given a cup of water to make him swallow. Balderdash! The person dispensing the medication could slip a few extras to a CMP who might be his favorite worker or an old buddy.

What's to say log entries weren't bogus. Written prescriptions were filled then filed away in the locked drug cabinet. That was accomplished by the Corpsman that happened to be in the treatment room. There was nothing to prohibit a doctor from gaining entrance to the locked cabinet, as well as civilian workers assigned to the medical department.

We had several CMP's assigned to Sick Bay. Most were lifers waiting for their appeals to end then transferred to a prison in their home state. For the most part, they were considered trustworthy, but many times that trust was taken for granted. Who wouldn't
trust a murderer in prison?

Mood enhancers were most useful in curbing manic aggression between inmates by stabilizing CMP's that were somewhat mentally deficient.

Prisoners did not run rampant. Quite the difference, voluntary movement by a CMP inside the Navy prison did not exist. The prescribing of mood stabilizers did not play a role in the daily operation.

The point is that in prison, the inmates will find away. The breach is terminated only for another infraction to materialize.

Contraband is the result of the prisoner's clandestine hush-hush proficiency to obtain an illegal item or substance using adeptness and know-how. Target areas; Sickbay, Library, Movie Theater, Work Area, Counseling Sessions, and Mess Halls serve as inspirations for the already known thieves.

You have been in the Marine Corps for a year or more and hold the rank of Private or Private First Class. You're assigned to guard, the worse of, the worse at the Castle. Could you be intimidated? Could you be used? Could you be scared? You bet the sweet ass you could, and the CMP gang leaders knew it.

Let's bring sex into the equation. Convicted Homosexuals were housed in the cells of the top tier. As directed by the mental health professionals, they were assigned to sickbay and other clerical staff offices for their work details. It provided an abundance of office nooks, empty rooms, closets, and storage areas for privacy. Daily lines of CMP's enter in these departments for administrative activity, medical concerns, educational projects, religious requests, and other various undertakings concerning the welfare during the CMP's incarceration.

    Who knows? This is a prison, and sex is sex. It was no secret that Gang leaders used weak CMP's as their servants and "sex slaves." I mean, what's to rule out staff or guard involvement? Contraband changes hands and favors granted. I heard but never knew factually, that the prison doctors confidentially treated CMP's that were sexually an assaulted

    The prison library possessed a large number of paperback books. Prisoners could check out a book to read during their off-hours. The books were all censored to ensure that reading material available assured officials that the contents were religious, nonviolent, and served as a medium for educational improvement.

    I believe I still have a paperback packed away somewhere that I appropriated for a souvenir. The title was the life story of the musical conductor Leonard Bernstein. When you opened the cover, you found the complete works of Marquis de Sade.

Chapter 8

I am going on my memory here. The straight and narrow CMP, which encompassed seventy percent of the inmate population, were allowed to receive five letters a week and could write out about the same. The CMP, who was borderline on being a goody-two-shoes, was limited to three letters in and out. The bad dudes got one. Real bad dudes got none. The same principle applied to magazines, books, and other mailings.

A memory came to me. Around the prison, you would hear the CMP's refer to "Splibs" and "Splib-Dudes. I may have it wrong, but if you were black, you were a splib-dude; if you were white, you were a splib. The terms interjected in everyday conversations by CMP's

Incoming letters would contain snapshots of girl friend's, wife's or relatives. Each CMP was allowed to keep three prints in his possession. When he received more than the allotted amount, he had to turn in his excess photographs. Photos were pre-censored and could not be traded or swapped. At mail call, the CMP may receive a standard mimeographed form that he had received two photos. However, the only one passed censorship, the other he would receive upon his release. Mail that did not pass censorship landed in the CMP's discharge box.

The term Semper Fidelis is a Latin phrase that means "Always Faithful." It is the motto of the U.S. Marine Corps. A rephrasing by the Marine Prison Guards translated to:

"If you fuck with one of us, you're fucking with all of us."

Let's pick up with that CMP who told a guard if he went back to Vietnam; he would most likely come back in a box.

The CMP was thoroughly disciplined, and the situation was old hat. MAYBE!

The mail orderly notes a letter addressed to the prisoner who was the smart mouth about Vietnam and coming home in a box.

Inside the letter was three photos' of a well-endowed young lady that showed it all except for the hair.

As the story goes, the guard in the mailroom lets his buddy know that the CMP who had pulled his chain received a weighty perfumed letter with photos that he should see.

At mail call, the CMP gets his mail, along with a standard mimeographed form, informing him that he received three photos, but only two-passed censorship. The one other he would receive on his release.

Back in his cell, the CMP couldn't take his eyes off either photo. He reads and re-reads the letter.

Dear Miles,

I have often wondered what became of you? You graduated joined the Navy, and that was the last I ever saw of you. I work at the Sears store on University Drive. Come to find out the lady I work with is your very own mother! She confided in me how the Navy blamed you for an incident that you had nothing to do with, then sent you to the Navy prison in Kittery.

I am going to visit my aunt in Portland for a few weeks, and maybe we could arrange a visit. My address is on the envelope. I hope you don't mind my racy photographs, but you can see I have grown out big time. Hope to hear from you. Your mom says, hi. Linda

He tried to remember her, but nothing was registering, who in the hell was Linda? What a body! She was going to make one hell of a welcome home present. Hornier than a two peckered mountain goat, he doles out three pages of unmitigated bullshit. In the morning, he would start the process of requesting a visitor. No doubt about it, he would be the envy of every fucking CMP in the prison.

He's surprised by receiving first-class mail service but pays it little attention. His top priority is fantasizing about Linda and her humongous tits.

Meanwhile, he submits an official request to have a visitor. No problem, it sails through the prison hierarchy without a hitch, even though to have a visitor a pristine good conduct record is mandatory.

The CMP was elated, not one of the dumb assholes signing his request took the time to check out his prison record.

The visitor's shack consisted of a cottage type building, located just outside the fence. The visitors are welcomed and admitted entrance before the arrivals of the CMP's. Inside the prison, the CMP's are lined up and inspected to their general overall appearance.

The Staff Sargent, in charge of the visitor's detail, slowly inspects each CMP from his toes to the top of his head. Satisfied, he executes a sharp turn to the right and inspects the next CMP. The anticipation of the CMP's is at an all-time high. They are only a few minutes from joining their visitors.

When the Staff Sargent reaches the next to last CMP, he makes his cursory inspection, except this time he orders the CMP to make an about-face, and remain at attention. The remaining CMP is inspected and approved. The Sargent orders his Corporal to move the detail to the visitor's center.

The CMP standing alone at attention is given the order to execute an about-face. He breaks the silence by asking the Sargent permission to speak. It is refused, and he is informed to keep his fucking mouth shut. Like a slow-moving turtle, it starts to sinks into the CMP mindset, that he is being duped.

The Sargent takes a stance in front of the CMP just a few inches from the CMP's face. He patiently waits for the CMP's adrenalin to move him from common sense to being pissed off.

"First of all CMP, the reason you're not at the visitors center playing footsy with your sweet thing is that your shoes look for shit. It will be noted that you weren't allowed a visitor privilege because of your unkempt appearance."

Standing at attention, the CMP knew that he was being fucked over. The Sargent makes a sharp turn and gives a command to his leading Corporal.

"Front and center."

As the Sargent leaves, the Corporal moves in very close to the CMP face talking just above a whisper.

"Well shit head, we had never met, I have served a tour in Nam and have orders to return. I am anxious to hear from a non-hacking, chicken shit, motherfucker, CMP, your theory on my coming back in a box."

The CMP remains poised but having increasing trouble keeping his being under control. The Sargent moves away, ordering the guard detail into his office. They will stay on duty until the visitor's hours are over.

The entrance of a Marine in his dress uniform, full medals, brass shined and wearing white gloves diverts the attention of the Corporal and the CMP.

The CMP recognizes the Marine immediately. The Corporal tells him to keep his fucking eyes looking forward. Without taking his eyes off the CMP, the Corporal speaks out to the visitor.

"You look sharp, Marine, what's the occasion?"

Without taking his eyes off the CMP, the Corporal speaks to the visitor;

"You look sharp, Marine, what's the occasion?"

Removing a photo from his pocket, he brings it up to his lips and plants a kiss on the front of it.

"I happen to know that this little beauty is far away from home and is sitting in our visitor's shack, sad, tired, and upset, wondering what is going on."

The Corporal nods his head in agreement but does not move his eyes off the CMP.

"The only CMP that missed visitors hour is the puke standing in front of me, and he's not going anywhere."

Moving to the side of the Corporal the Marine asserts himself in full view of the CMP.

The CMP hearing the Corporal knew he was being fucked over.

"I'm on my way to provide comfort and to be of assistance. The prison doctor, unfortunately, had to cancel her visitation. The CMP she was to meet has the flu, running a very high temperature and was placed in medical isolation."

All is going to plan. The CMP is feeling the phase of anger and hostility. Watching him closely the Corporal looks to any movement of his body.

I will console her disappointment with an explanation that I am wearing my dress uniform in anticipation of meeting my sister. "She was to arrive today, but car trouble has ended her trip. It seems as though we are in the same boat."

When she smiles and gives me a look of understanding. I make my move.

"I made dinner reservations for two at the Holiday Inn. Not to offend, I know you are greatly disappointed, but if you have nothing planned, would you take my sister's place and join me?"

I wait for her hesitation and continue.

"We could talk, and I could answer any questions you might have about your friend or the prison."

"She will nod her head in acceptance."
"I'm in!"

The Corporal laughing slaps his hands together while still maintaining a close visual on the CMP.

"A dinner will be a small price to pay just to get your hands on them big tits."

Holding his picture up to show the Corporal, he angles it so the CMP can see that it's Linda.

"I checked, and she has a room at the Holiday Inn for tonight. A few after-dinner drinks, and it's up to her room we go. I will lay back in bed with a glass of wine and watch her hum the Marine Corps Hymn on my bugle!"

The Corporal picks up on the sudden lunge forward by the CMP swinging a fist toward the front of his head. Using a counter move, the Corporal drops to a knee and flips the CMP over his body.

On cue, the Sergeants office empties

out, and within seconds the CMP is on the floor face down.

Chapter 9

The Sargent walks to the CMP, bending to talk to him.
"You assaulted a duty man. The guards will sign reports to witness that fact. You will have the opportunity to refute this claim, but not until you come out of the hole. Assault on a guard gets you a mandatory ten days of piss and punk."
The CMP tries to mumble, the Marine holding the back of his head forces his mouth against the floor.
The Sargent barks out an order.
"Corporal take this CMP down to the dungeon and see to it that he's made comfortable."
Immediately the Corporal gives the word to the guards holding down the CMP to drag his ass to the dungeon. The Sargent returns to his office, knowing that his actions left the CMP with little reprisal.
Released from solitary, the CMP is afforded a hearing before the disciplinary board to plead his case.
He accuses the guard that he had a previous altercation with, was out "to get him." Further, he

stated that the same guard knew he was part of the visitor's detail. Immediately after failing the so call bogus personnel inspection, he claims that the same guard appeared wearing his dress uniform.

He taunted me, saying that it was to bad my visit was canceled. Waving a photo of my girlfriend that I could plainly see, he laughed, saying he was on his way to the visitor's shack to ask this poor lonesome girl to join him for dinner. Then looking directly at me, he started describing how he was going to get her to perform oral sex on him. I lost my self- control and struck out at the first person in front of me."

The CMP was excused and taken back to his holding cell to await the board's decision. Once the CMP was dismissed, the board turned to the prison staff for there accountability.

CMP's working in sickbay told me that in this stage of the investigation, every CMP in prison knew the fix was on. The duty officer on the day of the incident stood before the board and read his prepared report.

He stated that a duty sergeant with eight selected guards had been assigned to the visitor's detail. Each of the board members were handed paper reports containing written statements submitted by the duty sergeant and all eight guards. All denied seeing a guard in his dress uniform.

The duty officer also stated that the CMP was held back from visitation due to his unkempt appearance. He violently resisted attacking the duty Corporal. He was subdued and placed in solitary confinement.

The duty officer reported that he had investigated the activity of the guard during the time of the CMP accusations. He handed each member, documentation from the manager of the J.M. Fields Department Store, that the guard was a part-time employee, clocked in, and was working at the time of the incident.

The board was dismissed after finding the CMP guilty of striking a guard. The CMP's charges had no substance and awarded him thirty days to be added to his sentence, loss of good time, housed in the cellblock, and to receive only minimal privileges until released.

The prison grapevine describes the board as just another example of military justice bullshit. Not enough to rebel or show a force of discontent. With only three or four months to go, CMP's were not about to raise any concerns over some shit head in the hole So much for brotherly love.

The game continues. Some of it is true, well somewhat true. Some are hearsay with stories and events that prisoners related to me. It would be hard for me to prove anything. It's the best of my recollections. However, I do stand by incidents and occurrences that I witnessed.

A good story going around might be true, maybe not. What to hell, you went ahead and believed it anyway. You had to remember it's a prison, hearsay supplied entertainment. A guard getting even could very likely happen. The mail orderly could have acquired Linda's name from a previous mail. It could be that Linda never existed! The letters and photos to the CMP may have originated inside the mailroom.

It may be very possible that the marine guard and the mailroom orderly instigated the whole smear for their entertainment. Then again, the mail orderly could have acquired the photos from the CMP's letter. Meaning, the story was created for one reason, and that was for revenge.

Regardless, the CMP had ten days of bread and water to think about it. Released from the hole, he soon found out that he was shoveling shit against the tide. They had nailed his ass. The prison CMP's would see to his comfort and needs, all he could do was to sit and stew until released.

Chapter 10

Chapter 10

You ask?

"What in the hell is the Dungeon all about?"

Below the prison was a big old underground cellar that, in all aspects, would meet the definition of a dungeon.

I remember two cells, but I'm sure there were more. The cells were constructed using cement blocks then coated with a coating material, I think! I didn't like it down there. There was a small viewing window built into each cell door. A heavy windowless steel door served as the entrance to the "hole."

Each cell was equipped with an iron rack (bed) cemented into the floor, a thin rubber mat, blanket, and pillow. I don't remember seeing a commode; I was told that there was a six-inch hole in the floor for the excrement of human waste. Once a day, the guard would flush it down with a pail of water. It could be true, my only view of the cell was from the outside passageway.

The daily ration was a quart of water and a loaf of bread. A corpsman had to be present to ensure the prisoner received his total allowance. I would be shown the loaf of bread and the quart of water, however, which was the end of my involvement. If a CMP had a medical issue, he had to be examined by one of the prison doctors.

A maybe storyline as if the CMP was hostile and unruly the cell door was opened, the loaf of bread was split in half, and the water poured into the bread. The soggy mess was then thrown into the cell, and the door slammed shut. I can't say I ever saw it happen, but I wouldn't doubt it for a minute.

Most CMP's when their time was up in solitaire, never wanted to opt for another tour. They expressed the desire to be good little boys, do their time, and leave.

The greatest story ever, concerning a CMP's confined to the dungeon, was about a CMP who, as fast as he was released from the hole, ended right back in it.

Time spent in the hole does not count as time served. This CMP didn't seem to let that fact concern him in the least. He weighed about one hundred and twenty pounds and stood around five feet two inches. No matter what they did to the poor bastard, they could not get him to say he was sorry.

The solitary unit was run by one mean, black gung ho, Warrant Officer. I met him just once, long enough to know he was one badass Marine, and no one to fuck with. He wore dark-framed glasses and kept his hair in a short wavy top

The story goes that the Warrant had just about enough of this piss ant prisoner who was making him look bad. He took a position in front of the cell door and ordered the guards to bring the CMP out.

Standing straight up in front of the Warrant, the CMP was a straggly, disheveled, sorry-looking piece of shit. The Warrant was in his face.

"Have you learned your lesson, boy?"

The CMP was maybe an inch shorter than the Warrant was quick with his response.

"Fuck you! You Sammy Davis Jew looking, motherfucker."

Then spit in the Warrant's face.

Unfortunately, the story ends there. True or false? I would have to lean toward it being greatly exaggerated but a top-notch prisoner's yarn of adulterated bullshit that will forever remain gospel within the prison walls.

What transpired after the incident?

The reaction of the Warrant Officer? The fate of the CMP?

The grapevine passed the word that it was another case of sick military justice. Covered up, the truth would never be known.

Now, if the hole didn't bring you to your senses, then there was always "Little Siberia." Little Siberia was a small chamber located inside a military bunker that might have been an extension of Fort McClary.

Guards told me that in the old days, the bunker was fortified to prevent enemy ships from entering Portsmouth harbor. An abandon ammunition storage bunker was refitted to serve as a solitary holding cell.

The main feature was that a heating system had been installed for use during cold months. The talk goes that in the winter, the guards would turn the heat down, and in the summer, when the cell was unbearably hot, the guards would turn the heat on.

I never got actually to enter the cell. When a prisoner was sent to Little Siberia for solitary confinement, a prison doctor was required to make a daily check on the prisoner's well being.

I want to substantiate that even though this is a really fun place, that disciplinary incidents actual or not, represented a small percent of the prison population.

Chapter 11

The New England State Prisons Association established a program where personnel from one state prison would travel and tour a neighboring state prison. The Navy Prison was involved in the program.

The primary reason for the visits was to introduce guards and staff personnel to a new prison environment, inmate-training programs, general living conditions, and a review of the emergency and security systems. Six marines and I boarded a small bus and set a course for the maximum prison at Walpole, Massachusetts. Upon arrival, the driver was directed to park in a secured parking lot away from the main entrance building.

Approaching the front of the building, we were led inside to a visitor center. Told to empty our pockets and to leave them inside out. Security officers checked our persons for contraband or items that could be changed in composition for a particular purpose.

Mainly a Weapon.

Pat down concluded we were asked to present our military ID cards to verify our individual identities.

Asked to take seats, we were welcomed by a Walpole senior guard. His presentation touched upon the fact that Walpole was not a military-run institution, and we would note the furnishings of some individual cells. Inmates earned these concessions by maintaining exceptional personal behavior, taking and completing various educational programs, and leading a no-violent lifestyle while serving their sentences.

Those that resist and push the envelope you will find in the tiered cellblock very similar to your own. You will witness that many inmates have some freedom of movement and are not required to follow painted lines. You are free to speak to an inmate and ask any questions. When you enter the facility, a guard that will be your tour guide will greet you.

You will keep him in your sight at all times. If he gives you a warning or an order, you are to follow it immediately. For your safety, I want to remind you again, this is a maximum prison. There are many evil people inside. Always be alert during your visit.

We were led through the building toward the entranceway to the main gate. Approaching a door, it opened, and we entered into a much smaller room. The door closed behind us, we stood facing a closed the door on the opposite side of the room.

That door opened, and we passed through arriving at the main gate leading to the prison. Later on the drive back to Kittery, we determined that in the small room, we were under security video and audio surveillance.

At the gate, instructions were given concerning our crossing the yard. From the gateway to the entrance to the prison were two permanent horizontal boundary lines, separated by a five to six feet cement walkway. Under no circumstances were we to step off the walk. We

formed a straight line and crossed the yard in the center of the sidewalk.

Security fences circled entirely around the prison. They were gruesome-looking, having a makeup of barbed and razor-sharp Constantine wire atop of the electrified fencing. I was sure that there were concealed electronic tripwires that would trigger various anti-personal devices. However, the guard assured us, "no claymores."

There was just no way a prisoner could ever make his way through that entanglement without serious injury.

During our tour, we were told that escapes had been tried. There had been several attempted escapes, but I could not verify that an inmate tried to escape by going over or under the wire. The guard suggested we change the subject as most of the information concerning escapes was highly classified.

Once inside the prison, we again showed our ID's and were logged in. We met the guard who was to be our tour guide. He was in his senior years, heavyset and definitely of Irish descent. He began telling us how he started out being a guard in the old Charlestown Jail.

"Now that was a prison, if a Con gave you any shit there, it became the worst day of his life. Yes, sir, those were the days, not like this chicken ass place."

After explaining why there were six Marines and one Sailor, we began the tour. First was a visit to a cellblock consisting of inmates who were in cells that were described to us by a previous guard. It was still prison but they had the privilege of having a television, coffee pot, writing table, reading material and during the day their cell door is unlocked.

One inmate we were conversing with asked us where we were from in which we replied the Naval Prison.

"I have done time in a couple of joints on the west coast and now I'm in here. Let me tell you the toughest can I was ever in was your Naval Prison. I got busted out of the Navy and did six months up in Portsmouth."

He was elated in telling us why.

"The damn place was run by you ass hole marines. That's what we called you in those days. Five o'clock in the morning it was junk on the bunk. Anywhere you went you had to follow the yellow brick road. You couldn't eat without some one yelling in your ear. The
stairs were torture and they made you run. It was a god dam zoo compared to here. Man I hated that place."

Thanking him for his ton of bull shit our guide led us through the different areas to the largest cellblock. Twice the size of the Castles. I couldn't guess how many cells there was and our guide's reply was that there was a shit load. Here the inmates had far less privileges than the first area we visited. We visited several of the prison workshops and ended up in the guards dinning room for lunch.

Through lunch the red-faced Irishman never stopped telling us about the good old days in Charlestown. He bitched about Walpole but every inmate in the place seems to know him and he referred to many of the inmates by their first names. He delighted in telling them they wouldn't last a day in the old Charlestown Jail.

After lunch he informed us that he would show us a cell where its occupant was murdered and the killer never found!

We entered a secured area but my

recollection of structural details is vague. It was the cell where Albert DeSalvo the Boston Strangle was found murdered.

We were shown to an entrance door and as I remember it had a small plate glass window for viewing. Upon opening that door there was a small space and another identical door. That was as far as we were allowed to go.

Peering through the windows you could see down a hallway with cement walls on both sides. The end of the hallway a solid wall had a showerhead extending from it. To the right of the shower we were told was an isolated cell. The guard on duty electrically operated the cell door.

The day in and day out routine was mundane. Once a day, watching through the window the guard would open, the cell door the prisoner would step out and stand beneath the shower. The water was turned on and I assumed the guard also controlled it. Showered the prisoner returns to his cell. The cell door is closed and locked.

I was told that for his meals the first observation door would be opened, the guard would step in with the door closing in back of him. He than would open a secured slot at the bottom of the second door that would allow him slide a prepared meal through onto the deck of the hallway.

I don't remember seeing it. Securing the open slot the procedure would be reversed with the guard out and both observation doors secured.

surveillance. He then returned to the cell and the cell door locked.

If I remembered just half of information correctly, how in the hell was he murdered in his cell?

"It had to be an inside job!"

The Irishman laughed.

After a through investigation the crime still remains unsolved.

Touring the recreational yard the smiling Irishman ask if we would be interested in visiting the death house? We quickly agreed.

The death house as the guard referred to it was a building located a short distance from the prison. During the short walk his stories continued to flourish. He had witnessed surveillance. He then returned to the cell and
the cell door locked.

If I remembered just half of information

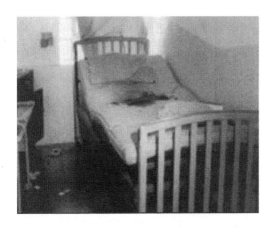

correctly, how in the hell was he murdered in his cell?

"It had to be an inside job!"

The Irishman laughed.

After a through investigation the crime still remains unsolved.

Touring the recreational yard the smiling Irishman ask if we would be interested in visiting the death house? We quickly agreed.

The death house as the guard referred to it was a building located a short distance from the prison. During the short walk his stories continued to flourish.

He had witnessed four or five executions when the chair was the old Charlestown Jail.

All he had to do is sit, watch the current hit the poor slob and leave. For that he got twenty-five dollars and the next day off. He related that in those days that was some deal for doing nothing.

Approaching the entrance he stopped us to explain strict procedures we had to follow.

"First of all the room is sound proof. On the other side of the wall is where the death row inmates are kept. Those sorry bastards are waiting for the State to decide if they are going to reinstate executions.

When we enter the room, I am asking you to be extra cautious of any sounds you might make. They can't hear us, but any loud noise that they can listen to makes them extremely nervous about what's going on? We try not to disrupt their lives, they have enough to worry about."

We entered the room in complete silence. The chair sat in the center of the room. Off to the side was a viewing room separated from the chair by a large glass panel. Our guide in a low voice explained the procedures that are followed as the inmate is placed in the chair and prepared for the electrocution adding that In Massachusetts, it takes a Master Electrician to throw the switch. Gathering us around the chair, he named the prisoners that he had watched meet their master as the electrical volts passed through their bodies.

He invited each one of us to go ahead and sit in the chair. All respectfully declined. Repeating the invitation, he emphasized that very few people would ever have the same opportunity.

Quietly he motions to me to have a seat.

"Show these marines what real sailors are made of."

The marines join in.

"Go ahead doc, sit in the chair, chicken shit squid. The bad mouth continued until I moved to the front of the chair and sat down. I didn't notice the guard moving behind the chair. He bent down and yelled, "BOO" in my ear while simultaneously poking his index fingers into each side of my rib cage.

I was stunned, scared shitless, and sat there shaking like a leaf. The marines watching my transformation to terror were cracking up in fits of laughter. It was a good ten minutes before everyone settled down including me.

I had been set up. There was no death row, no prisoners on the other side of the wall; it was used as a storage area. There is no death sentance in Massachusetts.

Since then I learned that the chair has been dismantled and destroyed.

For me, **I will never forget that grinning Irish son-of-a- bitch!**

Chapter 12

Somewhere along the line, the Command's name changed from the U.S. Naval Prison to the U.S. Naval Disciplinary Command.

Receiving orders to report for duty at the U.S. Naval Disciplinary Command, no one paid much interest until bringing up its old name, the Naval Prison.

It was not long after being station inside the Castle that the name "Disciplinary Command" began to fester into a king-size irritation.

What were the logical reasons for the name change? It did not require a brain surgeon to compile reasons to that effect. The very first logical answer would be in the posting of mail.

Ms. Jones receives a letter from her son via the mailman, who hands Ms. Jones a letter with a contemptible expression. Ms. Jones, I noticed Billy is in the Naval Prison. Ms. Jones turns abruptly and goes into the house. Mailman smiles and spreads the word.

However, the pseudo-intellectuals have an answer for Ms. Jones and her little Billy doing six months for stealing from his fellow ship-mates lockers and going AWOL.

Ms. Jones, a letter from Billy. I see he is stationed at the Disciplinary Command, may I ask where that is? It is a training facility. He has completed his GED and working on getting a Navy Certificate, validating him as an apprentice in metalwork. You must be proud, Ms. Jones, Billy is learning a trade and does not have to worry about Vietnam. Ms. Jones shakes the mailman's hand and starts to enter her house. She sees two Marine Officers, in dress uniforms, across the street knocking on Mrs. Smiths' door. Psychiatrists and psychologists were the convincing force behind the premise that the CMP's were not to blame for there confinement but the result of various early childhood traumas. Reinforcements to aid a pathway back to reality included light-duty, added privileges, weekly therapy, and anti-depressants.

This course of treatment may have been derived from the theories on behavioral sciences by Carl Jung and Sigmund Freud. Not from the teachings of the Holy Bible.

My way of thinking was that the CMP had to take a most realistic approach to self-examination, responsibility and each day add to his moral growth. Inmates that were strong in their religious beliefs unequivocally understood that they and no one else was responsible and accountable for their actions. They looked to the future, knowing they would have a cross to bear.

Our daughter was allowed inside the prison to make her Confirmation alongside several prisoners. There was some good

The name change from Naval Prison to Disciplinary Command, relieved the inmate from emotional and psychological stress from the stigma of the word "prison." Good for them.

It is storytime.

A former CMP goes for a job interview. The interviewer notes that the subject was in the Navy.
Interviewer: "Thank you for your service," what was your last duty station?
Answer: The Naval Prison, Kittery, Maine.
Interviewer: receive an honorable discharge?

Answer: No, I Received a Bad Conduct Discharge?
Interviewer: Security will escort you to the way out.

A former CMP goes for a job interview. The interviewer notes that the subject was in the Navy.
Interviewer: Thank you for your Service, what was your last duty station?
Answer: The Naval Disciplinary Command.
Interviewer: Was that like a Brig?
Answer: No, the Disciplinary Command was not a Brig. It was an institution devoted to trouble marines and sailors who receive guidance, maturity, and skills to use in civilian life.
Interviewer: What was your role there?
Answer: I received my High School GED and a certificate of training in the manufacture of clothing. It was a most rewarding experience and the reason I want to be part of your manufacturing force.
Interviewer: Very good, Honorable discharged?
Answer: Yes. (straightforward lie)
Interviewer: I am going to turn you over to our leading supervisor. He will brief you on our four-day workweek, salary, bonuses, benefits, paid holidays, sick leave, vacations, etc.

Interviewer: I see you were in the Service. What was your last duty station?

Answer: My last duty station was with the Third Marine Division in Vietnam. I was wounded three times, awarded three Purple Hearts, two Bronze Stars, a silver star, and the Medal of Honor. Discharged, I returned home.

Interviewer: What did you do there, your position, and what training you might of, received.

Answer: I was a designated infantry rifleman. My training was limited explicitly on how to kill the enemies of America using the most efficient weapons available.

Supervisor: As the senior manager of this company, we thank you for your sacrifice, dedication, and Service to America. Unfortunately, we have no job opening at this time. My daughter works at a McDonalds; I could have her talk to her boss.

My stories now hold no weight. A employer can no longer ask about your military discharge in an interview.

Chapter 13

I do have a recollection of a CMP who went on a hunger strike for reasons that the grapevine alluded to was in protest of the Vietnam War. I am not sure, but what else was there to protest. Poor bastard had it hard.

A good ninety percent of the prison population and I am projecting that high, based on my bullshit conversations with the CMP's were supporting the hunger strike.

I mean, what did they expect? They had a warm bed to sleep in, three meals a day, earn a GED, awarded training certificates for on the job training, medical and dental care, modern movies, local civilian entertainment, hot water showers, sanitary bathrooms, hair cuts, laundry service, visits with loved ones, time off for good behavior, free ride home, religious freedom, daily mail, and a free psychological evaluation.

Protectors of America what did you get mud fucking in the Jungle?
You got the Monsoons, Viet Cong and the North Vietnam Army.

The Naval Prison was under Marine command.

When in Vietnam, I was under Marine command.

Vietnam Holiday Routine; C-rations for supper, a rubber lady to sleep on, and a fifty-five-gallon barrel, cut in half, filled with diesel oil, to defecate in.

Only twelve months to go! My Morning Prayer, "I will probably die tomorrow.

I believe in the United States of America. In the first grade, I learned the Pledge of Alliance by heart. My father, my uncles, my aunts went to War during the 1940s. Why? Inspired by their peers, it was their obligation to defend our freedoms.

In my wildest imagination, could I have ever said, "I am not going."

Damn, I am digressing away from the title of the book.

Return to the hunger strike.

What I do remember are CMP's telling me that the splib dude on the hunger strike, was well educated and very intellectual. His parents had substantial influence and wealth. The CMP was not berthed in sickbay and perhaps housed in one of the isolation cells. The doctor wouldn't tell us. The only other location left would be a room in Officers country, but that was a long shot.

Here I go again off subject, but I have to tell you about Officers sentenced to do time at the Castle, housed in a private section of the prison. They had rooms and private messing facilities. They wore a khaki uniform, not a prison uniform. If they required medical attention, a prison doctor had to exam them in their quarters. Here is the best part? They had weekends off!

I mean Liberty call in downtown Portsmouth, New Hampshire.

"Hey, sweet thing."

Beyond what any of us thought, the hunger strike was lasting too long. The inmate was dangerously close to the state of no return. Refusing nourishment, his health was deteriorating rapidly.

An unexpected development occurred when his father and mother were stopped at the main gate to the Naval Ship Yard. They were insisting that they see their son and that their doctors examine him.

The request denied a vigil formed at the main gate. The parent's telephone calls opened up the incident to the public. Soon crowds were forming outside the gate, waving signs and demanding that his parents be allowed to see their son. As the word spread, the supporters grew in numbers.

Most surprisingly was the arrival of Doctor Benjamin Spock, renowned baby doctor and pacifist against the Vietnam War.

The pleas from the parents continued to be denied. The gate remained closed.

From here on out I am only relating to you what I was told by CMP's detailed to work in sickbay. Information was being passed from prisoner to prisoner, to every part of the prison. The grapevine was hot to trot.

Yes, CMP's are prone to lie a lot, and their stories may be true or false. No way of proving it. In prison, you are limited to two choices, believer or non-believer.

THE CMP feeding the grapevine information on the hunger strike inmate situation is unknown but has to be close enough to the setting to spread a believable rumor.

The Colonel heading for the cell block area is big news, and spreads through the institution like a wildfire. His destination is the cell holding the prisoner on a hunger strike.

Sitting alongside the inmate's bunk bed, he leans forward and speaks close to the inmate's ear.

The Chaplain, Doctor, along with two other staff members and for reasons unknown two Trustee's, entered the cell. The Colonel's message altered each time it was repeated on the grapevine. However, this is the version we got in Sick Bay.

"You are close to dying. The doctor has reported that vital signs are significantly abnormal.

Death is inevitable if fasting continues." The CMP opened his eyes and looked to the doctor, who shook his head in agreement.

"Your mother and father are gathered with many supporters at the main gate to the shipyard. They are demanding they be allowed to visit. That is not going to happen. The order has been given that the main gate is to remain closed. Soon death will call inside this cell. I have given orders that no one is to prevent it. I am going to let you die."

"The doctor will record the death as self-inflicted, then place a call to the county coroner. He will permit the local funeral director to put you in a body bag and deliver you to the local government contracted funeral home; they will have the discretion of when your parents can view your body."

When the Colonel rose to leave, he addressed the CMP one last time.

"There will be no last-minute rescues; you are on your deathbed. If you're a Christian, I suggest; you make your peace with God.

Giving the doctor instructions to notify him when the inmate expired he left.

Only a few minutes passed, and the

CMP motioned for water. The ordeal was over. He had enough intelligence to know that if left to die, his death would prove absolutely nothing and cause much grief for his parents.

That was one hell of a story, but being a corpsman and a Naval Hospital less than ten minutes away, the doctors would not of let him die in prison. They would insist on his transfer to the Intensive Care Unit for voluntary or involuntary treatment to sustain his life. He was still the property of the United States Government?

His parents and Dr. Spock at the main gate presented the possibility of a major public relations issue.

At a meeting of the minds, the discussions focused on how to make the CMP give up his fasting? The plan was developed and carried out to perfection. So well orchestrated that the CMP, his parents, supporters, and the population of the prison, went for it hook, line and sinker. So well done that it saved a life, calmed all involved, leaving the officials of the prison smelling like a rose.

Completing his sentence, the CMP was released and went on his way to achieve the American dream. (Obtainable by the sacrifice of American hero's that ensured his rights to do so.)

Chapter 14

There was only the talk of one escape during my tour of duty. Two CMP's assigned to work in the clothing factory were able to make themselves dark blue trousers and work shirts, resembling uniform work clothes. With nifty type logos just above the shirt pockets, they gave the appearance of being state employees. Black belts, work boots, and military looking ball caps completed their appearance.

Next, with help from the carpenter's shop came a wooden tripod and a replicate of a surveyor's site scope. A wooden pole painted with graduated black markings became the surveyor's sight pole.

Fellow corpsmen and sickbay CMP's told the same story that the two slowly made their way up through the prison yard.

One sighting in and the pole man was making white chalk Xs on the pavement. Still in the middle of the yard and directly opposite of the main entrance, the sight man aimed for the center of the gate.

A marine sentry approached them and asked what they were doing? The answer was that the prison was going to get a new gate or the pavement was going to be re-coated.

"They don't tell us much, we were told to survey and mark our centers, from the inside of the prison yard to the Shipyards main gate. That's all we know. I informed Cpl. Williams earlier when we checked in.

The sentry affirmed that the Cpl. had done so, and he was only verifying the information. He was quick to correct them; they had spoken to Cpl. Williamson.

'Hey, I'm sorry it was early, I was half asleep, it was Williamson, I've met him before when we sited out the new fencing. We have to sight out two more spots, then with the gate open, we can mark the dead center in the middle of the gate, and be out of your way.

The sentry opened the gate!

At the afternoon prisoners count, two inmates were missing.

A couple of months later, they were arrested in Texas. One of them just had to see his old girlfriend; local law enforcement was waiting.

Now that I have repeated the story, I have to believe it wasn't true. The sentence for escaping, when caught, was five years added to your sentence. It didn't make sense to trade four or five months for five years. However, their capture, and return to the prison were so factually reported I had to wonder?

Frank Napolitano, 85, of Somersworth, NH the oldest at the prison guard reunion, was at the Castle from 1949-1950. Napolitano recalls the time five prisoners escaped from the Castle. Four were soon found at a diner in Hampton.

One of the guards called in to search said he found the fifth guy in a car in a swamp in Hampton. I saw someone wearing the blue sweater they all wore. I think he was just as glad. It was pretty cold, and he was pretty tired and miserable.

Another guard recalled the time two prisoners escaped and were found minutes later at a bar in downtown Kittery. "I guess they needed a beer," he said with a laugh.

Others recalled the time some Marines and Navy sailors dusted it up inside Gilley's Diner when it was located in front of North Church in Portsmouth, and tipped it on its side.
Deborah McDermott SeaCoast.com

For the 66 years it functioned, any prisoner who escaped was brought back dead or alive so it has been said.
Katy Kramer "Portsmouth Naval Prison"

JAIL BREAKER KILLED.

Portsmouth Navy Prison Guards Wound Two More—They Will Recover.

PORTSMOUTH, N. H., Jan. 28.—While attempting to escape from the naval prison here in a boat to-day, three men were shot by armed guards, who killed one fugitive and wounded the other two. The dead man is R. F. Spurling of Indianapolis. The wounded men are Harry McGarvey and Albert J. Montgomery, homes unknown. Both will recover.

The men were serving short terms for minor offenses at the navy yard prison. At the end of the noon hour, when the prisoners in detachments of about a dozen each, were marching back to their places of employment in the yard, the three men made their dash for liberty. Breaking from the ranks they scudded for the gates. A momentary impulse on the part of the rest of the detachment to follow was frustrated by the accompanying guards, who closed in on them, leaving the escaping trio to other guards.

The sounding of the jail-break signal on the fire alarm whistle brought every guard in the yard to his post. Nevertheless, the fleeing trio by dodging around various buildings managed to reach the banks of the Piscataqua River and jump into a skiff which they found there. Guards followed fast upon their heels, and the fugitives had gotten only a few hundred feet out into the stream when the pursuers, seeing their demands for surrender disregarded, opened fire.

Spurling almost immediately fell into the bottom of the boat with a bullet lodged over his heart.

A moment later McGarvy fell, shot in the breast, and a bullet went crashing through one of Montgomery's arms. The boat drifted helplessly about the river with its wounded crew for some time before the guards could put out and tow it back. The wounded men were sent at once to the Naval Hospital for treatment.

Chapter 15

POTPOURRI

DISCHARGES

Not so honorable enlisted discharges. What in the hell is a BCD? (Bad Conduct Discharge.) At one time in this country, it meant the kiss of death. Today its one of several discharges that the public and military people are no longer familiar with or care about, Undesirable Discharge, General Discharge, Other Than Honorable Conditions Discharge, Medical Administrative Discharge, Entry Level Separation Discharge, and Dishonorable Discharge?
All these discharges are available to any American Citizen who doesn't mind letting some one else defend his rights.

Officer discharge
 Commissioned officers cannot receive bad conduct discharges or a dishonorable discharge, nor can they be reduced in rank by a court-martial. If an officer is discharged by a general court-martial, they receive a Dismissal notice, which is the same as a dishonorable discharge. Would the average

Personnel Director know what a Dismissal Notice represents?
CAN'T ASK

Due to legal issues surrounding Equal Employment Opportunities and related laws, one has to be careful in the interview process. It is illegal to ask which type of discharge a military veteran received.

IF I WAS THE SUPREME COMMANDER THE MASTER OF THE UNIVERSE 1. The six-month sentence would be history. If our fighting troops have to spend a year in combat, then a quitter should spend a year in the joint. 2. No CMP noon meal! Lunch consisting of a C-ration, limited to Ham and Lima Beans with Pound Cake.
!The Marine Corps Hymn alternates every hour over the loud speaker system with Anchors Away, 24/7 365 days a year
A big sign at the front gate "No Shrinks*

BALDERDASH!

In the 1973 movie The Last Detail, Seaman Larry Meadows (Randy Quaid) is escorted by

Petty Officers Billy "Badass" Buddusky (Jack Nicholson) and Mule Mulhall (Otis Young) escort Larry Meadows (Randy Quaid) to the Portsmouth Naval Prison. Meadows has been sentenced to 8 years of confinement for trying to steal $40 from a charity box. But because of his harsh sentence, the guards feel sorry for Meadows. They decide to show the naive sailor the time of his life before arriving on Seavey's Island (where another location substituted for the actual prison).
Wikipedia.org Portsmouth Naval Prison

The prison is referred to in Stephen King's 1982 novella The Body, later filmed as Stand by Me. The prison and shipyard locations were used to depict a Russian shipyard in the 1978 TV Movie The Defection of Simas Kudirka starring Alan Arkin.   Wilkipedia.org Portsmouth Naval Prison

Actor Humphrey Bogart, however, probably does have ties to the prison. He apparently was on his way there with a prisoner, who, at one point, smashed him in the mouth and tried to escape. It's unknown whether Bogie actually made it to Kittery.
Seacoast.com

Walt Disney never served a prison sentence at the Portsmouth Naval Prison, even though local legend has it that the castle-like quality of the building served as his inspiration for the Magic Kingdom.

Local building contractor and developer Joseph Sawtelle estimated the cost to renovate the immense edifice into civilian office space, including removing lead paint and asbestos, would cost more than $10 million.
Seacoast.com

TIDBITS
The Vintage News by Brad Smithfield
    Don't be fooled by the prison's seemingly appealing look from the outside. The real horrors came from the inside, which is how the place earned its formidable reputation as a dangerous and menacing spot, with a secretive nature.

    When the war was over, Portsmouth housed the surrendering German crew of four U-boats. They were treated harshly while there, and the correctional officers looted all of their possessions. Reports say that the German commanding officer, Friedrich Steinhoff, was even pushed to the point of committing suicide. It was only after he was transferred to Charles Street Jail that he did it slitting his wrists with broken glass. When officials found him, it was already too late. He died on his way to the Massachusetts General Hospital.

Contrary to popular belief, Portsmouth was actually modeled after Leavenworth prison in Kansas and Auburn Correctional Facility, New York, not Alcatraz.
Sep 26, 2017, Brad Smithfield

NOTATION

Before there are shouts of plagiarism for using other people's research, let me give credit where credit is due. I identified most in the pages of the book.

GaryHildreth, PublicAffairsOfficer, Portsmouth Naval Shipyard - Inmate training

J. Dennis Robinson; "Heavenly Days at the Hellish Portsmouth Naval Prison."

https://en.wikipedia.org/wiki/Portsmouth_Naval_Prison

http://www.seacoastonline.com/article/20141208/NEWS/141209387

http://www.seacoastonline.com/article/20141208/NEWS/141209387

Deborah McDermott
1908 to 2008 Shipyard Historical Foundation

Katy Kramer "Portsmouth Naval Prison"

Boston Globe - Albert DeSalvo

"A History of the US Naval Prison"
Portsmouth, New Hampshire
100th Anniversary
 Portsmouth Naval Prison
1908 to 2008
Written by Robert J. Verge
Lieutenant (S), USNR
Education and Training Officer

     I was given this publication by Ross Freeman, an excellent friend who had gone with one of his friends to the 100th Anniversary Reunion. Knowing I had been stationed there, he brought back an incredible history of the Naval Prison written by Lt. Robert Verge. Courtesy of Portsmouth Naval Shipyard Historical Foundation.

The prison closed in 1974 but still stands erect on the shores of the Atlantic Ocean. Deemed a Historic Landmark, it cannot be altered or demolished.

The Portsmouth Naval Prison, built to be a modern correctional facility for a navy, which had once disciplined by flogging and capital punishment, was rendered obsolete. After containing about 86,000 military inmates over its 66-year operations, the prison closed.

USS NEW HAMPSHIRE (SSN-778) Virginia-Class Nuclear-Powered Attack Submarine passing the US Naval Disciplinary Command.

Edward T Duranty is from the White Mountains of New Hampshire. Graduated from Whitefield School and enlisted in the U.S. Navy. He served aboard three ships, the Naval Hospital, Newport and as a Combat Corpsman with the 3rd Marine Division, Vietnam. He attended and received his BS degree at Salve Regina University. He is a member of the American Legion, Veterans of Foreign Wars and the Disabled. American Veterans.

He and his wife Elaine, live in Englewood, Florida |

Frank Napolitano, 85, of Somersworth, NH, the oldest at the prison guard reunion, was at the Castle from 1949-1950. Napolitano recalls the time five prisoners escaped from the Castle. Four were soon found at a diner in Hampton. One of the guards called in to search said he found the fifth guy in a car in a swamp in Hampton. I saw someone wearing the blue sweater they all wore. I think he was just as glad. It was pretty cold, and he was pretty tired and miserable.

Another guard recalled the time two prisoners escaped and were found minutes later at a bar in downtown Kittery. "I guess they needed a beer," he said with a laugh.

Others recalled the time some Marines and Navy sailors dusted it up inside Gilley's Diner when it was located in front of North Church in Portsmouth, and tipped it on its side.
Deborah McDermott SeaCoast.com

For the 66 years it functioned, any prisoner who escaped was brought back dead or alive -- so it has been said.
Katy Kramer "Portsmouth Naval Prison"

Chapter 15

POTPOURRI
DISCHARGES

Not so honorable enlisted discharges   What is it with a BCD? (Bad Conduct Discharge.) At one time in this country, it meant the kiss of death. Today its one of several discharges that the public and military are no longer familiar with or care about, Undesirable Discharge, General Discharge, Other Than Honorable Conditions Discharge, Medical Administrative Discharge, and Entry Level Separation Discharge. Dishonorable Discharge is perhaps the most noteworthy.

Officer discharge

 Commissioned officers cannot receive bad conduct discharges or a dishonorable discharge, nor can they be reduced in rank by a court-martial. If an officer is discharged by a general court-martial, they receive a Dismissal notice, which is the same as a dishonorable discharge. Would the average Personnel Director know what a Dismissal Notice represents?

CAN'T ASK

Due to legal issues surrounding Equal

Employment Opportunities and related laws, one has to be careful in the interview process. It is illegal to ask which type of discharge a military veteran received. (perks for the draft dodgers, politicians and presidents.)

IF I WAS THE SUPREME COMMANDER

1. The six-month sentence would be history. If our fighting troops have to spend a year in combat, then a quitter should spend a year in the can.
2. No CMP noon meal! Only lunch consisting of a C-ration, limited to Ham and Lima Beans with Pound Cake.

SHIPBOARD

On my ship, the Commanding Officers policy, "If you can't behave and do your work, then I am not going to feed you!" Everybody ate....

Naval History and Heritage NH8 *82328
USS NAVAL PRISON 1910
(DO YOU THINK IN THOSE DAYS THEY KICKED SOME ASS?)

Guards in summer uniforms armed with shotguns. The Portsmouth Naval Prison, built to be a modern correctional facility for a navy, which had once disciplined by flogging and capital punishment, was rendered obsolete. After containing about 86,000 military inmates over its 66-year operations, the prison closed.

USS NEW HAMPSHIRE (SSN-778) Virginia-Class Nuclear-Powered Attack Submarine passing the US Naval Disciplinary Command.

BALDERDASH

In the 1973 movie The Last Detail, Seaman Larry Meadows (Randy Quaid) is escorted by

Petty officers Billy "Badass" Buddusky (Jack Nicholson) and Mule Mulhall (Otis Young) to the Portsmouth Naval Prison. Meadows has been sentenced to 8 years of confinement for trying to steal $40 from a charity box. But because of his harsh sentence, the guards feel sorry for Meadows. They decide to show the naive sailor the time of his life before arriving on Seavey's Island (where another location substitutes for the actual prison). Wikipedia.org Portsmouth Naval Prison

The prison is referred to in Stephen King's 1982 novella The Body, later filmed as Stand by Me. The prison and shipyard locations were used to depict a Russian shipyard in the 1978 TV Movie The Defection of Simas Kudirka starring Alan Arkin. Wilkipedia.org Portsmouth Naval Prison

Actor Humphrey Bogart, however, probably does have ties to the prison. He apparently was on his way there with a prisoner, who, at one point, smashed him in the mouth and tried to escape. It's unknown whether Bogie actually made it to Kittery.
Seacoast.com

Walt Disney never served a prison sentence at the Portsmouth Naval Prison, even though local legend has it that the castle-like quality of the building served as his inspiration for the Magic Kingdom.

Local building contractor and developer Joseph Sawtelle estimated the cost to renovate the immense edifice into civilian office space, including removing lead paint and asbestos, would cost more than $10 million.
Seacoast.com

TIDBITS

The Vintage News by Brad Smithfield

Don't be fooled by the prison's seemingly appealing look from the outside. The real horrors came from the inside, which is how *the place earned its formidable reputation as a dangerous and menacing spot, with a secretive nature.

When the war was over, Portsmouth housed the surrendering German crew of four U-boats. They were treated harshly while there, and the correctional officers looted all of their possessions. Reports say that the
German commanding officer, Friedrich Steinhoff, was even pushed to the point of committing suicide. It was only after he was transferred to Charles Street Jail that he did it, slitting his wrists with broken glass. When officials found him, it was already too late. He died on his way to the Massachusetts General Hospital.

Contrary to popular belief, Portsmouth was actually modeled after Leavenworth Prison in Kansas and Auburn Correctional Facility, New York, not Alcatraz.

Sep 26, 2017 Brad Smithfield

NOTATION

Before there are shouts of plagiarism for using other people's research, let me give credit where credit is due. Most I identified in the pages of the book.

GaryHildreth, PublicAffairsOfficer, Portsmouth Naval Shipyard - Inmate training

J. Dennis Robinson; "Heavenly Days at the Hellish Portsmouth Naval Prison."

https://en.wikipedia.org/wiki/Portsmouth_Naval_Prison

http://www.seacoastonline.com/article/20141208/NEWS/141209387

http://www.seacoastonline.com/article/20141208/NEWS/141209387

Deborah McDermott
1908 to 2008 Shipyard Historical Foundation

Katy Kramer "Portsmouth Naval Prison"

Boston Globe - Albert DeSalvo

"A History of the US Naval Prison"
Portsmouth, New Hampshire
100th Anniversary
Portsmouth Naval Prison
1908 to 2008
Written by Robert J. Verge
Lieutenant (S), USNR
Education and Training Officer

    I was given this publication by Ross Freeman, a good friend who had gone with one of his friends to the 100th Anniversary Reunion. Knowing I had been stationed there, he brought back an excellent history of the Naval Prison written by Lt. Robert Verge. Courtesy of Portsmouth Naval Shipyard Historical Foundation.

The prison closed in 1974 but still stands erect on the shores of the Atlantic Ocean. Deemed a Historicandmark, it cannot be altered or demolished.

Books by Edward T Duranty

NEWPORT
NEWPORT 2

WILFRED THE DEVIL'S DISCIPLE
SAMUELL OWENS THE PIG BOY
A SAILOR CAME TO NEWPORT
ME- VITAMIN E- MOSES AND LUCIFER
BILLY ONE EYE
USS ASPRO (SS 309)
SLAUGHTER IN THE TRAILER PARK
TRUTH BE KNOWN
THE SCAMMING OF MACBETH
      (Four-Act Play)

AVAILABLE AT CREATE SPACE
PARENT COMPANY
WWW.AMAZON BOOKS. COM